W9-BIJ-572

What Is the Difference between Clouds and Fog?

by Kristen Pope

E 551.57 .POP (handwritten)

Published by The Child's World®
1980 Lookout Drive • Mankato, MN 56003-1705
800-599-READ • www.childsworld.com

Acknowledgments
The Child's World®: Mary Swensen, Publishing Director
Red Line Editorial: Editorial direction and production
The Design Lab: Design

Photographs ©: iStockphoto, cover, 1, 9, 10, 12, 14, 15, 21;
Alexander Chernyakov/iStockphoto, 5; Ian Chris Graham/
iStockphoto, 7; James Anderson/iStockphoto, 17; J. DawnInk/
iStockphoto, 19

ISBN 9781503807945
LCCN 2015958201

Printed in the United States of America
Mankato, MN
June, 2016
PA02299

ABOUT THE AUTHOR

Kristen Pope is a writer and editor with years of experience working in national and state parks and museums. She has taught people of all ages about science and the environment, including coaxing reluctant insect-lovers to pet Madagascar hissing cockroaches.

TABLE of CONTENTS

CHAPTER 1

What Is a Cloud?

Some days, the sky is blue and empty. But other days, it is full of clouds. Clouds come in many forms. Some are high and wispy. Others are fluffy. They look like cotton balls. And some clouds look flat and low in the sky.

Clouds are made of water. All around us, there is **water vapor** in the air. It is a gas. A gas is a form of matter that expands. It fills the space it is in. Most of the time we can't see water vapor. But when it goes up high in the sky, it can change. Up high, the air gets cooler.

Clouds can come in many shapes and sizes.

Then the water vapor in the air **condenses**. It turns into drops of water.

When the water drops stick to **particles** in the air, clouds form. Clouds are made of water drops. Clouds can be very, very high up in the sky. It is very cold that high up. Sometimes the water drops in the clouds freeze. Then the clouds are made of ice crystals.

When enough drops come together, they can make rain. The cloud gets heavy with water. It cannot hold more droplets. Big drops fall from the sky. If it is cold enough, the drops will freeze. They fall as snow.

When clouds get too heavy, rain starts to fall.

CHAPTER 2

What Is Fog?

Fog can make it hard to see. Sometimes it can be so foggy you can't even see across the street. Like clouds, fog starts out as water vapor in the air. Most of the time you can't see water vapor.

Sometimes the weather is **humid**. This means there is a lot of water vapor in the air. This can make it more likely that fog will form.

Fog forms when the water vapor becomes cool. This causes it to condense. The water droplets stick to particles in the air. This makes fog.

Fog can make it hard to see buildings.

Fog is similar to a cloud. But it is very close to the ground.

Fog forms closer to the ground than a cloud does.

There are many different kinds of fog. One kind happens on cool, clear nights when humid air gets chilled. The water vapor in the air condenses. Then fog forms.

Another kind of fog is caused by warm air on top of a cold surface. This can happen in the winter. Warm air is above cold, snow-covered ground. The cold ground cools the warm air right above it. Then the water vapor condenses.

Sometimes, when it's very cold out, the water droplets from fog can freeze to surfaces. This can make ice. These icy surfaces can be dangerous. They can make roads and sidewalks slippery.

Fog can form in winter when the air is warmer than the ground.

In the fall or winter, fog can make lakes look as if they are steaming. This is another kind of fog. It is caused by the cold air above the warmer water. Water from the lake **evaporates**. It becomes water vapor. Then the water vapor rises up into the cold air. It condenses back into water drops. Then fog forms.

In very humid places, fog can last for days. Other places are very dry. They do not get much fog at all.

Fog can be dangerous. But it can also be useful. People can catch fog. They turn it into water. Some ancient cultures put big pots out under plants when it was

Fog can look like steam rising up from a lake.

foggy. The water droplets from the fog would collect on the plants. Water would drip into the pots.

Even today, some people use fog catchers. These are big screens that catch the water droplets. The water drips down. It is collected below.

Water droplets can collect on leaves when it's foggy.

CHAPTER 3

What Is the Difference between Clouds and Fog?

Clouds and fog are both made of water vapor. In some ways they are the same. But in other ways they are not.

Clouds are found all around the world. Some places get more clouds than others. But many places do not get much fog at all. Valleys and spots by the coast can get a lot of fog. But some places get just a few days of fog each year. Many desert areas do not get much fog.

Clouds can form all sorts of shapes. Some are fluffy. Others are thin and

Seattle gets a lot of fog.

wispy. Sometimes a cloud will look like a dog or a bird. But fog does not usually make shapes. Fog can be thick or thin. When it is very thick, people sometimes say, "This fog is as thick as pea soup!"

Clouds and fog also form at different distances from the ground. Fog is low to the ground. Sometimes clouds can be miles up in the air. The highest clouds can be over three miles up in the sky.

Fog forms when the air near the ground is cool. Then the water vapor in the air turns into water drops. Clouds form when the air high in the sky is cool. This turns the vapor into water or ice.

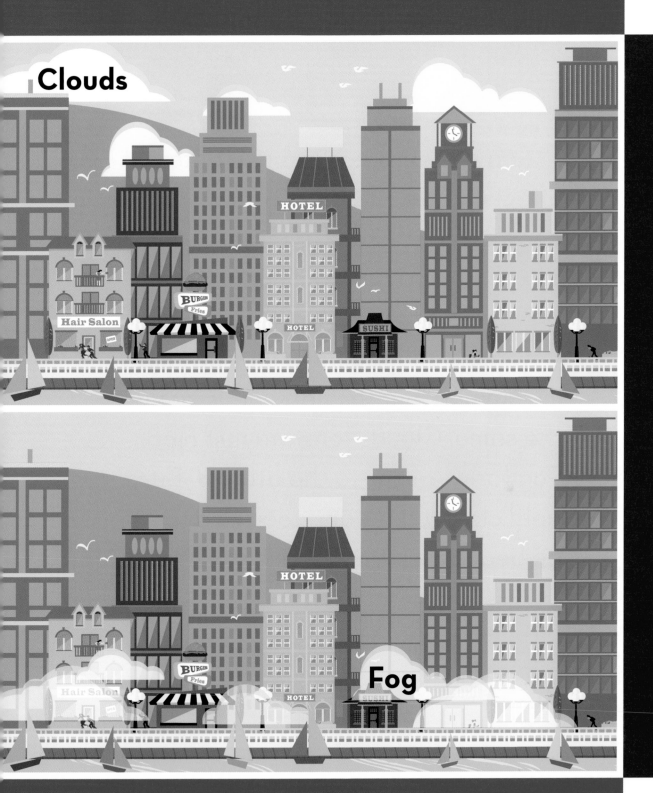

Clouds

Fog

Clouds form high up in the sky. Fog forms close to the ground.

Fog and clouds also have different effects on **visibility**. On a cloudy day, people can still see for miles. But on a foggy day, people can only see short distances.

Clouds and fog have many things in common. But they are not exactly the same. Clouds form way up high. Fog forms closer to the ground. But both cloudy days and foggy days can be beautiful!

Even when there are clouds in the sky,
it's easy to see long distances.

Fog in a Bottle

You can create your own fog at home.

What You Need

Water

Clear jar or bottle

Plastic bag

Ice cubes

What to Do

1. Have an adult help you heat up the water and pour it into the jar or bottle. Leave it there for 60 seconds.

2. Have an adult pour out most of the water.

3. Place a plastic bag filled with ice cubes over the top of the jar or bottle.

4. Watch fog start to form inside!

Glossary

condenses (kun-DENS-ez) When something condenses, it turns from a gas into a liquid. When water vapor in the air cools down, it condenses to form water drops.

evaporates (i-VAP-uh-rayts) When something evaporates, it turns from a liquid into a gas. When water in a lake evaporates, it rises up into the air as water vapor.

humid (HYOO-mid) It is humid when there is lots of water vapor in the air. Humid air can produce fog.

particles (PAR-ti-kuls) Particles are tiny pieces. There are particles of dust in the air.

visibility (viz-uh-BIL-i-tee) Visibility is the ability to be seen. Fog can cause low visibility.

water vapor (WA-ter VAY-per) Water vapor is water that has been heated up enough to turn into a gas. Water vapor is always in the air.

To Learn More

In the Library

Bauer, Marion Dane. *Clouds*. New York:
Simon Spotlight, 2016.

Delano, Marfé Ferguson. *Clouds*. Washington, DC:
National Geographic Children's Books, 2015.

Rockwell, Anne. *Clouds*. New York:
HarperCollins, 2008.

On the Web

Visit our Web site for links about clouds and fog:
childsworld.com/links

Note to Parents, Teachers, and Librarians: We routinely verify our Web links to make sure they are safe and active sites. So encourage your readers to check them out!

Index